Praise for

THE CONTRARIAN SALESPERSON

"A simple yet powerful blend of selling disciplines from which the most seasoned sales professional will benefit."

—**Dave Jenner,** SVP Sales and Marketing,
Maurice Sporting Goods

"There is nothing 'contrarian' about the success my sales teams have enjoyed by following Jody Williamson's advice and guidance. This book explains those methods perfectly in a readable style."

—**Kevin Grogan,** CEO, Flexible Packaging,
DS Smith Plastics, North America

"A must-read for sales professionals and executives who want to reach their full business and personal potential. *The Contrarian Salesperson* provides a clear and practical road map to success."

—**Markku Kauppinen,** President and CEO,
Extended DISC North America, Inc.

"Whether you are refreshing tired sales skills or beginning your professional sales journey, Jody Williamson's *The Contrarian Salesperson* provides you with eight powerful principles that will move you towards sales success."

—**Dean Dietrich,** VP and General Manager,
Consumer Packaging Group, Caraustar

"Jody Williamson has boiled down the eight essential principles used by the highest performing salespeople to excel. The compelling and powerful lessons contained in this book can transform any sales professional's life and income."

—**Ken Harris,** EVP Sales and Marketing,
Pelstar LLC/Health-o-meter® Professional Scales

"If you are a salesperson, and we all are, the question is, 'How do you attract, rather than chase?' *The Contrarian Salesperson* offers a unique story that answers that question."

—**Lee Brower,** Founder, Empowered Wealth, LC,
The Business Family Coach®

"Definitely a book I would want the sales team and other managers in my business to read."

—**Jeff A. Christensen,** VP and General Manager,
Sonoco Alloyd

THE
CONTRARIAN
SALESPERSON

THE
CONTRARIAN
SALESPERSON

A Parable for Non-Traditional Selling

JODY WILLIAMSON

Sandler Training

Paperback ISBN: 978-0-692-62524-8
E-book: ISBN: 978-0-692-62525-5

sandler.com/contrarian-salesperson

To Virginia and Bob Williamson,
the best parents any son could ask for.

To Deb, for your ongoing support and love.

To Ben, Logan, Audrey, and Tess,
for your constant inspiration; you are all uniquely gifted,
and I'm so proud to be your father.

CONTENTS

FOREWORD

I n *The Contrarian Salesperson*, Jody Williamson offers a first—an easy-to-read, lightning-fast, fictionalized business parable based on the core principles of the Sandler Selling System® methodology.

When Jody first proposed this idea to me, I was intrigued and curious about what it might actually look like in print. No Sandler® author had attempted anything like this as a book project. After two years of work, the final product is finally ready for prime time, and we couldn't be happier. In the pages that follow, you'll find a timeless story that brings to life, in a compelling way, eight of the most important Sandler principles. It's a major contribution to the growing genre of "success fiction," and an exciting new point of entry to the selling system developed by our company's founder, David Sandler.

I think Jody should be proud of the result. I certainly am.

David H. Mattson
President/CEO, Sandler Training

"Whenever you find yourself on the side of the majority, it's time to pause and reflect."

—MARK TWAIN

PROLOGUE

The Memo

E ven before he caught sight of tiny-eyed, red-haired Paula Procedure from HR waiting for him in the conference room, Alan sensed this was not going to be a good meeting. Paula clutched the special black clipboard she only used during discussions about employee termination.

Like a hungry vulture, Paula leaned her small red head forward and scanned her familiar territory, sizing up the corpse that didn't yet know it was a corpse. She stared at Alan with a smug, patient expression on her face—as though she had all the time in the world.

It was official. The next half-hour now had "crash and burn" written all over it. There was no use pretending otherwise. The memo Alan had gotten that morning from his boss, Harvey Hardnose, had been proof enough of that.

To: Alan Atleaster

From: Harvey Hardnose

Regarding: Your sales production

Meet me at 9:30 A.M. sharp in Conference Room A.

Harvey

Alan, a salesperson for Acme Corporation who prided himself on his ability to talk his way out of anything and who is a former Rookie of the Year, was now enduring the worst stretch of bad luck of his four-year career. This was saying something. After his stellar first season, Alan had no shortage of bad luck.

Alan hadn't hit his sales quota for six consecutive quarters.

He had come close to quota a couple of times over the past year and a half, which he felt should have counted for something. But he had still been put on a 30-day probation. Then he had lost his biggest account.

None of that (he had been preparing to explain to Harvey) was really his fault.

Here is what Alan had been all ready to say to his boss before he stepped into that conference room.

Harvey, you know and I know that the economy as a whole has been wildly unpredictable, and our industry has suffered a severe setback due to turbulence in some key industries. All of that was in *The Wall Street Journal.* I'm not making that up. It's a fact. Not only that, but budgets are tight right now. Everyone is cutting back and making price the issue, not just for us, but for everybody trying to sell in this space. You know that, too. What's more, everyone goes through a slump now and then. I'm not alone! So what we are looking at now is a transitional period. Anyway, the whole industry is down and the market is bad. But that will change eventually. We all know the competition is undercutting us right now. If the competition weren't so brutal, I would have hit quota in two or maybe three of those quarters. Let's not forget my territory. It is legendary for being hard to sell. As for the leads, they are garbage, and you and I both know that is the truth. If I had better leads, Harvey, I'd be back on top in no time. Let's face it. What we sell has become completely commoditized. The occasional bad quarter is inevitable because this game is all about price now, and there really isn't anything either of us can do about that.

That was the speech he planned to give. It was a good one. Of course, Harvey would have a speech of his own, and Alan would be obliged to listen to it.

Alan had imagined that Harvey had scheduled this meeting to scare some sense into him. He was prepared for that. Alan didn't have any illusions about this being a pleasant discussion. But he had figured it would be over soon, once he had given his own little speech, and he could get back to calling the people on his "hot list." He knew the names on this list well because he called them often.

Contrary to what Harvey might imagine, Alan really was eager to get to work. So, he was interested in getting this meeting started, giving his speech, nodding his head as many times as necessary to get through whatever Harvey had to say, and moving on. In short, Alan was interested in doing what he did best: talking his way out of trouble.

Then he saw Paula.

Paula's sober gaze seemed to send him a silent message: *There will be no talking your way out of this one.*

•   •   •

A rumor of long standing within the Acme sales department had it that Paula Procedure took a special delight in firing salespeople. A recent rumor, equally popular, held that she had, over the decades, fired a total of 99 salespeople. Supposedly, she kept a running tally on a sheet posted on her wall.

Paula Procedure needed to fire one more salesperson

before she retired, the rumor went, in order to meet her personal goal of 100.

Whether this was true or not, Alan had no way of knowing. He did know that the sales team had bestowed on her a special nickname, one never repeated in her presence: the Angel of Death.

Paula lived to facilitate firing discussions. Her only possible function at meetings such as these was to advise you that you were about to be terminated and then to move the termination paperwork forward through the proper channels. Was it even possible that Alan had reached such a dangerous point without realizing it? Wasn't there supposed to be some kind of warning system?

"Hi, Paula," Alan said, taking a seat. "Do you know what this is all about?"

Paula grimaced, apparently intending this expression to pass as a smile. Then she looked away. She said nothing.

There was an increasingly uneasy silence. Alan pondered the tops of his shoes. Paula checked messages on her phone. The moment seemed to last forever.

Finally, Paula looked up and said, "Harvey just texted me. He's running late. He wants me to tell you that we both need to stay here until he shows up." She grimaced again, then looked away.

The Angel of Death was biding her time. It looked to Alan as though she were tracing the figure "100" in very large numbers, over and over again, on her legal pad. Whenever she caught Alan trying to sneak a peek, though, she changed the angle of the pad.

Alan waited. His stomach churned.

•   •   •

"Consider this your official termination," Harvey Hardnose said, striding into the room and handing Alan a sheet of paper bearing much tiny print. "Paula has been copied on this. She is serving as a witness to our discussion. As of today, you are terminated from the employ of Acme for cause, specifically for failure to perform up to the standards outlined in your employment agreement..."

And he left the terrible sentence hanging.

Harvey took a seat. He stared Alan down with eyes of steel.

Alan felt his heart racing. A deep emptiness settled over the conference room.

"...unless..." Harvey said.

"Unless what?" Alan said, after choking back a little gasp.

"Unless you agree to sign a revised job description requiring you to spend the next eight weekends, at a minimum, with your new coach, Carl Contrario."

"Carl who?" Alan stammered. "What kind of name is Contrario?"

"Never mind that," Harvey snapped. "Carl is a friend of mine from college. We were hired here at Acme at about the same time. He set every Acme sales record before he left to start his own company. He works as a consultant these days. All you need to know right now, Alan, is that Carl Contrario is the only thing standing between you and a pink slip.

"Now let's be honest with one another. I've been patient for the past year and a half, and I do like you a lot. You remind me of me at your age. You talk a good game. But I'm afraid I've run out of patience. No stories. No excuses. No promises. No doubletalk. Don't even try it, Alan. You'll regret it if you do."

Alan started to speak, but Harvey held up his hand, which stopped him. There was silence. Harvey opened a manila folder and extracted a second sheet of paper bearing much small text. He passed the sheet to Alan. It had a blank line at the bottom, awaiting Alan's signature.

"Here's what we're looking at. You either report to Carl Contrario at eight o'clock tomorrow morning and convince him that you're coachable, or I let you go. It's up to you, Alan."

"Tomorrow morning—Saturday? That's my golf day! I have my regular tee time tomorrow at eight o'clock."

The expression on Harvey's face made Alan wish he'd kept this observation to himself.

Alan noticed Paula smiling, as though she had somehow expected him to say something dumb at this moment.

"Are you interested or not, Alan?" Harvey waved a gold-plated pen at him to sign.

Alan thought for a moment, took a deep breath, accepted the pen (gold-plating and all), and talked his way out of trouble with a single well-chosen word: "Yes."

"Are you sure? I don't want you to do this unless you are totally committed."

"Yes, I'm sure."

After signing the sheet and returning it, and the pen, to Harvey, Alan Atleaster looked up and saw Paula Procedure's brows knit in disappointment.

The Angel of Death must have been hoping for number 100 today, Alan thought. *But she isn't going to get it. Not just yet.*

RULE 1

Zig When Others Zag

Murray, the cab driver, scowled a little when Alan read out the address Harvey had scrawled on a slip of Acme note paper. When Alan repeated himself, the cabbie shook his head, punched the number into the GPS, and started driving. Alan didn't like taxis, and these days he didn't like spending money on cab fare—he could barely afford his golf game—but his wife Kathy needed their only car on weekends to run errands.

"Rural neighborhood," the cab driver said. He muttered something unintelligible as he guided the yellow Crown

Victoria onto the freeway on-ramp leading out of town.

What Alan had expected to see was a shiny, modern office building. Yet when they finally arrived at their destination—ten minutes before Alan's appointed starting time—the spot didn't look at all like what Alan was expecting.

This was no office building. The place where the cab stopped didn't look like the lavish comfortable home of a successful salesperson, either, which was the second thing Alan had expected. After that long ride, which had culminated in a bumpy, bone-jarringly unpaved road lined with tall trees, the place where they finally stopped was a small, dilapidated trailer.

This trailer had been left, for reasons only it knew, in a small clearing in the middle of a dense stretch of woods serviced by one uncertain road. A mailbox, suspended uneasily upon a two-by-four someone had jammed into the soil, proclaimed, in white paint, the same address written on that slip of Acme stationery.

This was a weather-beaten, distinctly lonely-looking trailer. It had been out on its own for a long time. And it had seen better days.

Alan thought to himself: *I missed my tee time for this?*

"You sure this is where you're supposed to have your meeting?" Murray asked.

Murray was gruff and bearded, and his tone of voice suggested that he was wary of the surroundings. The place didn't look all that inviting to Alan, either. Three scruffy crows landed on the roof of the little trailer. They glared at Alan.

Should he stay or should he go?

Alan pulled out his phone and dialed Harvey's home number.

"What is it, Alan?" said Harvey, groggy, but apparently still able to make out the Caller ID readout. "I was hoping to sleep in today."

"Sorry," Alan said, "it's just that I think I must have written down the wrong address. The place the cab driver took me to is, um..."

"A ratty-looking old trailer?"

Alan was speechless.

"Yep," Harvey said. "That's his office. Trust me, where he actually lives is much, much nicer. I guess I should have expected your call. Carl Contrario does all of his consulting in that little trailer. It's part of the training. Wait. What time is it? 7:53 A.M. OK. Good. You're not late yet. Whatever you do, Alan, pay the cab driver and go knock on that door before it's eight o'clock. You do not want to be late with this guy. Good luck."

And Harvey hung up.

Obediently, Alan paid his fare and stepped out of the cab.

It pulled away in a yellow blur, picked up speed, and disappeared. Alone on the dirt road, Alan stared at the little trailer, then checked his watch.

7:55 A.M.

Quickly, he made his way to the door and knocked three times.

"Come in," said a man's voice within. He sounded relaxed.

Alan opened the flimsy-looking door.

> **contrarian** (adjective) Opposing or rejecting popular opinion; going against current practice.

To Alan's surprise, the interior of the trailer was—or at least appeared—sturdy, spacious, luxurious, tastefully lit, and quite well appointed. Some kind of optical illusion must have made the room look like that.

Half a dozen important pieces of pop art—seemingly genuine, although that hardly seemed possible—lined the walls. Alan thought he recognized, on the furthest wall, an Andy Warhol painting he had studied in his college art history class, *Dollar Sign*.

Beneath that spectacular image, behind a sleek mahogany desk, sat a thin man with a thin face in a dark business suit, middle-aged, with immaculately coiffed salt-and-pepper hair. He wore round John Lennon glasses and a white tie.

"Congratulations, Alan," the man said, gesturing toward a plush, leather-upholstered armchair positioned directly in front of his desk. "You've made it past the first level. Most people walk away before they've even said a word to me. You didn't make that mistake. But I suspect you called your boss to confirm you were in the right place. Didn't you? Hmmm?"

The clear eyes behind those Lennon specs stared at Alan without blinking.

Alan took his seat, then nodded.

"No matter," the man said. "You're here. Once you knock on the door and step in here before eight, all is well. But if you'd been late, oh, this would not have gone well at all. You'd have failed before we even spoke a word to each other! And you'd have lost your job—for *failing to be coachable*! By the way, one of the first things you will learn here is that the very best salespeople are the most coachable ones. They're coachable because they're always growing."

He laughed abruptly, stopped laughing just as abruptly, stood, reached over the table, grabbed Alan's hand, and shook it vigorously. "I'm Carl Contrario, Alan. Glad to meet you. You are coachable, aren't you?"

"I hope so."

Carl released Alan's hand and resumed his seat behind the desk.

"Can I ask you a question, Carl?"

"Sure!" Carl beamed. Behind the round lenses, his eyes radiated with what appeared to be genuine joy at having begun in earnest. "Sure! Ask away! Ask as many questions as you like! I love questions!"

He seemed to mean it.

"Well," Alan said, "I'm not sure how to put this, but—there's something about this room that feels odd to me. Maybe it's my imagination. Is this place bigger on the inside than on the outside?"

"Oh, it's not—not really," Carl said. "It couldn't be, could it? Don't worry about that, Alan."

Carl Contrario winked.

"I happen to have a great interior decorator," Carl continued. "She's marvelous. I think she must have meant for me to use the interior space here as some kind of metaphor."

"What metaphor would that be?"

"You tell me."

There was a silence. Alan thought for a moment. Then he said, "More than meets the eye?"

Carl clapped his hands.

"Marvelous!" he shouted. "Marvelous! Harvey finally sent

me a bright one! Someone who can actually think on his feet! Yes, indeed, Alan. There is more to you than meets the eye. Well done."

Alan, who couldn't remember saying anything about himself, took a deep breath. Things were getting stranger by the minute.

Fortunately, that deep breath calmed him down. Alan looked at Carl, who was once again smiling without a word for no apparent reason, and then he looked around the room, taking in all the rich details. His eye kept returning to that Andy Warhol painting: *Dollar Sign*.

"Can I ask another question?" Alan said.

"Sure!" Behind the steel-rimmed circles of glass, Carl's blue eyes looked like a happy child's. "You bet!"

"It's obvious you could afford a real office if you wanted to. Why the heck do you work in a trailer?"

"To keep people like you on your toes," Carl said. "To be unlike what you expect. Be honest. When your cab pulled up, you took one look at my little trailer, and you thought you were in the wrong place. In fact, you were certain you were in the wrong place. Why? Because you'd never, ever expect a sales mentor who is any good to deliver personal sales coaching in a dingy little broken-down trailer. Am I right?"

"Right," Alan agreed. "Is that what we're doing now? Personal sales coaching?"

Carl nodded, excited, and flashed another big grin. "Yep. That's what we're doing. In an environment you didn't expect. Truly effective selling is all about not doing what's expected. Now, before we get started, Alan, I want to set some ground rules that will help us work together."

"Sure—what are they?"

"If we're going to accomplish anything worthwhile, it's important that you be totally committed to making changes and to taking my coaching."

"That's why I'm here!"

"Yes. But everyone says they're committed, right up until the moment I ask them to change their habits. I guess I want to make sure you're prepared to make some big changes."

Alan nodded. "Yes. I am."

"Another thing: we're going to have a series of coaching sessions. I need to make sure you're agreeing to show up for all of them."

"Hmm," said Alan, pondering his weekly 8 A.M. tee time once again. "I thought maybe we'd meet a couple of times, get a whole lot done, and then, who knows, find a way to cover everything in a few weeks."

Carl shook his head slowly. "I can tell already," he said, "that we've got a lot of work ahead of us."

"Well," said Alan, "Can't blame a guy for trying. I'll be here. I'm ready to get to work."

"Are you sure you're OK with all of this? Because if you're not, that's fine. We don't have to do this."

"I'm sure. I definitely want to do this. I'm ready to roll."

"Let's get started, then. There are eight big principles I'm going to be sharing with you during our meetings. I call them Contrarian Selling Rules."

"Contrarian?" asked Alan. "What do you mean by that?"

Carl handed Alan a card, which Alan, eager to show how coachable he was, read out loud. Here is what the card said:

Zig when other people zag.

"The first Contrarian Selling Rule," Carl said, "is: 'Zig when other people zag.' Tell me, Alan: *Why* does a Contrarian Salesperson zig?"

Alan only had to think for the briefest instant. "Because everyone else is zagging?"

"Are you asking me, or telling me?"

"Telling you. They zig because everyone else is zagging."

"Yes!" Carl shouted, pumping both fists in the air. "You're going to get this rule down in record time, Alan. I just know it. By the way, that's how Warren Buffett became a billionaire. Zigging when everyone else was zagging. Warren Buffett figured out something important, something all Contrarian

Salespeople know: The fact that a belief or practice is popular or repeated frequently does not make it true, valid, or useful. You have to be willing to look at things differently.

"Think about what happens when a salesperson calls someone new on the phone to pressure that person to set up a meeting. The moment the prospect senses that pressure and realizes that a salesperson is on the phone, what does he do? He goes on the defensive. He shuts down. He withholds information. That pattern establishes itself predictably. If we're not going to fall into that pattern, we need to do something different than what the prospect expects.

> *"Think different."*
>
> **—STEVE JOBS**

"We are Contrarians, Alan. We are all about doing the opposite of what other salespeople do. Now why do you think that is?"

"Because...if you act like every other salesperson, you're going to be treated like every other salesperson?"

"Marvelous! We don't deserve to be treated that way, do we?"

"No," Alan said. "We don't."

"Glad to hear it."

Carl pulled out, from the top drawer of his desk, a pad of paper and a ball-point pen. He held them up for Alan's examination.

"To get our heads around the first rule," Carl announced, "we're going to start a game called Word Association. You'll be using these two simple tools to play. There have been a lot of game shows built on this over the years. You've probably seen some of those shows on TV. The host reads a certain word aloud, and the contestants say the first word that comes into their head. You know how that kind of game works, Alan?"

"Sure."

"All right," Carl said, handing over the pad and the pen to Alan. "But this version of Word Association has a twist. When I say the word, I want you to write down only what parents, relatives, prospects, and other authority figures, including TV producers and moviemakers, had to say about this word while you were growing up. Ready?"

Alan clicked the ball-point pen and positioned it over the paper. "Ready," he said.

"The word," said Carl, "is *salesperson*. You have two minutes. Start writing."

Eager to fulfill his coach's instruction, Alan set pen to

paper and began jotting down words. They came much easier than he imagined they would. At the end of the allotted time, he had written down a lot.

"Read to me what you've got," Carl said.

So that's what Alan did. Here's what his sheet said:

- Fast-talking
- Slimy
- Sleazy
- Dishonest
- Liar
- Insincere
- Snake oil
- Shady
- Slick
- Phony
- Two-faced
- Tricky
- Fake
- Self-serving
- Manipulative
- Misleading
- Shifty
- Slippery
- Out to make a quick buck
- Scumbag

Carl looked at Alan, smiled, and said, "With a reputation like that waiting for us before we even sell anything, do you ever stop and wonder why we went into this line of work?"

Alan smiled, too, but he said nothing.

"Believe it or not, those are pretty typical responses," Carl said. "There's a reason they're out there. Salespeople perpetuate these stereotypes. They've been doing it for years. Many don't level with people. They are perceived as untrustworthy, as emotional fakes. But that's not how I see myself. Is that how you want everyone to see you?"

"No," said Alan, without hesitation. (And it wasn't, either.)

"Good," Carl said. "Now the question is, what are you supposed to do when you deal with prospects or customers who do see you that way? We have to assume they got the same programming you did when you were growing up. How are you going to handle them, Alan?"

"I have absolutely no idea."

"You agree they do have preconceptions about you before you even reach out to them?"

"Sure," Alan said. "You can tell when people you meet are on their guard. You can tell when they don't want to be pushed around by a salesperson, and I don't blame them. I don't want to be treated that way, either, when I go shopping for something."

"Well put."

"So what's the answer?"

"Don't act like a typical salesperson," Carl said. "Ever. That's the ultimate expression of Rule Number One. If you notice the competition doing something, I want you to stop doing it. Right away. If you notice yourself sounding or acting like a typical salesperson, I want you to do something else."

"Wow." Alan frowned. This sounded suspiciously like unlearning everything he'd ever picked up about how to sell. "Do I have to do that?"

"Yep," Carl said. "It's the price of admission. If you see everybody else is zagging, you're going to have to learn to start zigging. If there's something you're comfortable doing but it's not working because everyone else in the marketplace is doing it, you're going to have to walk away from it. If you're not willing to commit to that much, we don't have a lot to talk about. That's why you're here today, Alan. To promise me you'll walk away from a habit when I say it's time to walk away. No matter how familiar that habit may feel to you."

Carl raised his eyebrows expectantly. This was, apparently, the moment of truth. Alan took a deep breath.

"OK," Alan said. "When you say it's time to walk away, I'll walk away."

"Now then, here's the biggest question of the day. Are you sure you want to become a Contrarian Salesperson? There's still time to back out. It's OK to say this isn't what you want to do. I don't want to put any pressure on you. I'm OK if we're done. I take rejection well. Are you positive you're ready for this?"

"Yes," Alan said quickly, imagining that Carl would call Harvey and report some serious uncoachability if he said anything else.

"Marvelous," Carl said. "Marvelous."

Everything in Carl's world, apparently, was marvelous.

"Now that you're a Contrarian Salesperson in training," Carl said, "you can expect to find your whole orientation toward prospects to change. You'll find it easier to say what you feel. Things that used to bother you will stop bothering you so much. Yes, prospects lie to us. Yes, they try to steal our expertise, pick our brains, pilfer our ideas. Contrarian Salespeople accept all that as part of the job. And why do we do that? What's the alternative? Resenting it? Doing what everyone else does, fighting prospects tooth and nail?"

"I guess you're right," Alan said, after a moment's thought. "That wouldn't make a lot of sense."

"Marvelous. You've done a great job so far, Alan." Carl pulled out his phone and texted a cab, requesting an early pickup. "I've taken the liberty of calling a cab for you. We're done for today. We'll cover Rule Two next Saturday."

"OK," Alan said, pondering his lost tee time. "I guess I was hoping we'd have gotten a little further today."

"You remember how, when we got started, I warned you that we wouldn't be able to do all of this quickly? Contrarian Salespeople zig when others zag in terms of their own professional development, too. That means we don't try to cover everything in one day or one weekend."

Alan nodded.

"You know how a lot of people go to a day-long seminar and think that one day is going to be the answer? They walk out all pumped up, but nothing really changes. By the next week, they are back to their old habits and behaviors. It's like trying to learn a foreign language in a one-day seminar. That's not how people change."

"Or learn how to golf," Alan added.

"Exactly. You're going to see that I'm all about the spaced repetition of learning, Alan. We learn something, we try it, we come back next week and talk about what we did. Then we try something new. Once we've mastered the skill, we pass it along to someone else. By the way, that's what you're promising to do by coming to these sessions every week. Master a skill and then pass it along to someone else. Deal?"

"Deal," said Alan.

SUMMARY

Carl Contrario's Wisdom in a Nutshell

- A Contrarian Salesperson zigs because everyone else zags.
- The fact that a belief or practice is popular or repeated frequently does not make it true, valid, or useful.
- In sales, as in other aspects of life, you have to be willing to look at things differently in order to produce a different and better result.

The Traditional Salesperson:

1. Acts like every other salesperson.
2. Gets treated like every other salesperson, and not in a good way.
3. Is inauthentic.

The Contrarian Salesperson:

1. Acts the opposite of every other salesperson.
2. Gets treated differently than other salespeople.
3. Says what he feels.

Carl's Question for You

- What changes do you need to make so that you are not perceived as the stereotypical salesperson?

RULE 2

Sell Adult-to-Adult

The next Saturday morning had not started out well.

Alan, unhappy at the idea of another cab ride, had asked to take the minivan. This had led to a squabble with his wife Kathy, who was used to having the car on weekends and wasn't about to cancel a couple of errands and a visit with her mother. They'd made up, but Alan had been relegated to the care of a wary cab driver once again. This one, Juanita, made pretty much the same face Murray had when she pulled up in front of the trailer and roared off even quicker once Alan had paid and stepped out.

All week, Kathy had been asking when they would buy another car—but until Alan got his sales numbers up, there seemed no point in reigniting that argument.

• • •

"I've been looking at the notes that Harvey sent along," Carl said, shuffling a few folders on his desk as they started their second session. He took a printed sheet from one of them and scanned it carefully. "One of the issues he's concerned about is the high number of quotes and proposals you are working on. Can you think of any reason why that would be a negative for him?"

Alan tightened his lips, drew in a deep breath, and made a mental note not to make any impulsive, knee-jerk replies. This thing about proposals was something Harvey had been whining about for months, and now it looked like Carl was in on the whining party, too.

"I really don't know," Alan said carefully. "I guess Harvey's got his reasons."

"Of course he does," Carl said encouragingly. "We've all got our reasons." He stared placidly at Alan, as though it were Alan's turn to speak.

Alan, however, could think of nothing intelligent to say. Nearly a minute went by in total silence. It felt like an hour to

Alan. He shifted uneasily in his chair. Finally, he said, "So...is there something you want to tell me about doing quotes and proposals?"

"Oh, no," Carl said. "Not at all. Not in the least. I'm here, first and foremost, to listen. But I do think there is probably something you want to tell me about quotes and proposals." Carl smiled.

"Can you give me a hint?" Alan asked.

"Hmm," Carl said, as though pondering a difficult math problem. "How many quotes or formal proposals would you say you've done over the past year?"

Alan thought for a moment. "Maybe fifty."

"About one every week."

"I guess so. Yes, figure in two weeks for vacation, and that's what the math looks like."

"Can I ask another question, Alan?"

"Sure."

"How many of those actually came through and produced revenue for you?"

"Um...you mean this year? One or two this year, but last year there were a few more."

Carl grimaced. "I see. Can I ask you something else?"

Alan nodded.

"How many requests for information or proposals have

you declined to respond to over the past year?" Carl asked.

After pondering the question, Alan said, "Zero. But that's only because I didn't want to miss out on—" But for some reason, Alan felt hesitant about finishing the sentence.

"Didn't want to miss out on what?"

"Well, I didn't want to lose any opportunities."

"You and I live in the real world, Alan. In the real world, you can't lose what you don't have."

Alan had never considered the matter from this point of view.

"So you have nothing," Carl said, his gaze steady. "They send you an email. They start issuing demands. What's really happening? You still have nothing. Only now, they're the Parent, and you're the Child. They're saying, 'We need your proposal or your information by such-and-such a date, and while you're working on it, you are forbidden to call us and ask us questions. Submit all your questions via email because we're very busy here. Do exactly what we say, from beginning to end. Then, if you're lucky, we'll tell you whether or not you are in the running.' Isn't that what's happening with most of the proposals and information you send out?"

Alan had no good answer. That was what happened. With all of them.

Carl continued, "The problem is, when most salespeople

see that a prospect wants information or a proposal, they get excited. Now, for one or two whole days, they get to work on a proposal! Instead of the horrible prospecting! Is any of this ringing a bell?"

It did. Alan said, "Yes."

"Then what happens? Most salespeople start jumping through all the hoops. That's what just about everybody in sales does. They turn into unpaid consultants. Is that what we want to do?"

"No."

> "Be yourself—not your idea of what you think somebody else's idea of yourself should be."
>
> **—HENRY DAVID THOREAU**

"Marvelous!" Carl said. "Coachability! I love it! That's a true Contrarian talking." The smile on Carl's face could have lit up Manhattan in a blackout.

"But I should point out," Alan offered, "that it's usually less formal, smaller proposals and quotes that I am generating. They don't take that much time to generate. After all, sales is a numbers game, right?"

"No," Carl said. "It's a peer-to-peer game, first and foremost. Guess what, Alan? It's not only proposals that turn us into unpaid consultants. The same exact thing happens anytime we make the mistake of thinking that our job as professional salespeople is to do whatever we're told to do by the prospect. Unfortunately, we do that a lot."

"Do we?"

"Of course we do. We do it just about every time the prospect says, 'Jump through a hoop.' The problem is, prospects ask us to jump through hoops without using those actual words. Usually, what they say sounds like this: 'Do a demo,' or 'Give us samples,' or 'Talk to our technical people,' or 'Do a proposal for us.' What do we do? We jump right through the hoop, every time, whatever it is. We do exactly as we're told, like a little trained dog. Whenever we do that, Alan, the prospect is up here—" (he held his hand above his head) "—and we're down there" (his hand dropped to the desk).

"They want to make you the Child, and they want to be the Parent. They want you to do whatever they ask you to do. They want to say, 'Jump,' and have you say, 'How high?' The minute you agree to that role, from that point forward, you will always be seen as a vendor, and not as what I like to call a 'Trusted Advisor.' You don't have to give them information just because they ask for it. Do me a favor. Write this down every day as a reminder."

Carl seized and uncapped a black marker. He wrote this in big letters on a sheet of paper:

Salespeople Have Rights!

"Salespeople who forget they have rights are known as 'vendors.' Unless I'm very much mistaken, you've chosen to be seen as a vendor many, many times. Am I right, Alan? Haven't you ever felt as though you were following someone else's lead, jumping through someone else's hoop? Haven't you ever felt like there had to be a better way?"

Alan took a deep breath—then nodded his head in silence.

"So now we know. We have to get away from the Parent-Child relationship, and we have to act like an Adult talking to another Adult. We have to create a relationship that's truly peer-to-peer, where both parties have equal business stature. That's our goal in every interaction, every communication, every discussion—whether it's face-to-face or virtual. Until we get ourselves into a habit of engaging in Adult-to-Adult transactions, we can't expect to create a relationship where we are seen as the Trusted Advisor. That's where we have to work from—the Trusted Advisor's space."

"What does being a Trusted Advisor have to do with selling?" Alan asked.

Carl rubbed his hands together. "I'll answer that question by posing another. Remember back to a time when you've had a big medical problem of some kind. Which did you want to see: A doctor with a degree? Or a guy who's thinking about going to medical school some day?"

Alan smiled. "The doctor, of course."

"Me too. Now, does a doctor jump through hoops for the patient?"

"No. If anything, just the opposite."

"Correct. At the very least, the doctor starts out on the same level with the patient, or even a bit higher. Am I right?" Carl held his two hands out, parallel to one another, then raised one hand a few inches higher than the other.

"Right," said Alan.

"Good. We agree. Now we know what a Trusted Advisor is."

"But help me understand something. Are you saying a Trusted Advisor never responds to requests for information?"

"No," Carl answered. "What I'm saying is that it's OK for you to respectfully decline to respond when it makes sense to decline."

Alan looked confused.

Carl smiled. "OK. Let me ask you something. If there were an opportunity for you to work together and you declined the offer to quote on something, wouldn't a real prospect—someone who actually wanted to work with you—look you in the eye and say, 'Hang on. What information do you need from me?'"

Alan pondered this. He was too embarrassed to admit that he couldn't even think of a time when he had respectfully declined to fulfill a request for information. He said, "Wow. I'll have to remember that. But what if they don't say that? I mean, what happens if I respectfully decline and they say, 'OK, goodbye'?"

"Then you had no chance to begin with. They were just looking for your information. Or they wanted you to give them a price they could use to negotiate with their current vendor. Or they were looking for some way to use your ideas so they could do the work themselves."

"But I don't want to lose out on any opportunities!"

Carl shrugged his shoulders and said, "You can't lose what you don't have. Last week, we talked about walking away from habits that make you look like every other salesperson. Remember?"

Alan nodded.

"This week we talked about something that most salespeople don't do very well, which is remember that they have rights, too. So what's Rule Two of Contrarian Selling?" Carl asked.

"If it's about not acting like the Child to their Parent," Alan said, "Rule Two is: 'Sell Adult-to-Adult.'"

"Marvelous!" Carl said. He clapped his hands together in authentic joy. "Now are you ready to take some notes?"

Alan nodded. For the rest of the morning, that's exactly what he did.

SUMMARY

Carl Contrario's Wisdom in a Nutshell
- Keep it Adult-to-Adult.
- You can't lose what you don't have.
- It is not the job of a professional salesperson to do everything the prospect says.

The Traditional Salesperson:
1. Acts like the Child to the prospect's Parent.
2. Does whatever the prospect asks.
3. Doesn't think salespeople have rights.

The Contrarian Salesperson:
1. Sells Adult-to-Adult.
2. Isn't afraid to respectfully decline.
3. Knows salespeople have rights.

Carl's Question for You
- What improvements do you need to make to be more Adult-to-Adult in your sales approach?

RULE 3

Everything Is an Iceberg

Alan, who was preoccupied, hadn't even asked his wife about using the minivan that morning.

In the cab on the way to the third meeting with Carl, Alan was worried about how he was going to say what he had to say. As he settled into his chair in Carl's office, Alan felt his stomach churn a bit.

Alan had barely taken his seat when Carl, jumping right into the discussion as though a week had not intervened, said, "How did that Adult-to-Adult thing work out for you?"

"Time out," Alan said. "I'm having a little problem here.

Can I ask you about something before we get started?"

"Sure," Carl said. "What's on your mind, Alan?"

"Well—is it OK if I take it slow with all this?"

Carl looked at him quizzically. "When you say 'take it slow,' what do you mean?"

"I work in a unique industry," Alan said, his eyes riveted on the floor. "I appreciate all you're doing here, and I'm sure a lot of this is going to end up being helpful to me. But the idea of coming out and telling prospects I'm not going to give them information—I wasn't able to do that this week. I can think of quite a few people I know who aren't going to react well to that."

"Hmm. You know that?"

"Yes."

"What happened when you did it?"

"Well—like I say, I didn't actually do it this week."

"So, do you *know* your prospects wouldn't react well to it? Or, do you *think* they wouldn't react well to it?"

This distinction hadn't occurred to Alan. "I guess I think they wouldn't."

"Right. Big difference. Yes?"

"Yes."

"So, what do you think? This week, will you walk away from that habit? Will you implement what we talked about last week? That way we'd know for sure."

This seemed fair enough.

"Deal," said Alan. "I'll give it a try."

"Did you ever see the movie, *The Empire Strikes Back?*"

The subject change startled him. "Yes. Why?"

"My favorite part is when Yoda says, 'Do—or do not. There is no try.'" Carl smiled that hundred-watt smile.

"OK, OK," Alan said. "I'll do it."

"Marvelous." Carl kept beaming. "To get your head around Rule Three, Alan, you're going to have to answer a riddle. Ready?"

Not wanting to come across as anything but coachable, Alan smiled and said, "Sure."

"How is a prospect like an iceberg?"

Alan thought about this for a moment, then said, in an uncertain tone of voice, "Profoundly cold—but susceptible to occasional long-term warming trends?"

Carl smiled again. "Interesting, but not exactly what I was looking for. Here. Take a look."

He produced, from somewhere beneath the desk, a stand-up poster that bore a drawing of an iceberg. The drawing looked like this.

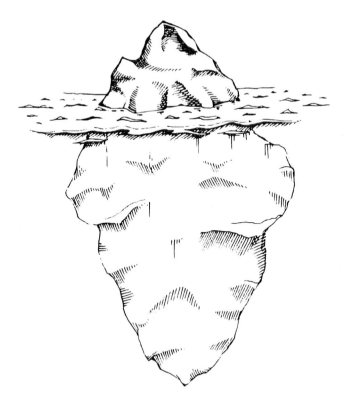

"Most of the salespeople I work with don't get what's most important about icebergs, either. Not at first. Take a close look, Alan. What's important about an iceberg?"

"Most of it is underwater."

"Marvelous!" Carl exclaimed. "That's exactly right. Most of the iceberg is under the water. Only the tip is visible from the surface of the ocean. Now, how do you think that relates to selling?"

There was a pause as Alan evaluated his options. "What you see is not all there is to see when dealing with prospects?"

"That's exactly what it means. Now, how would that affect you as a salesperson?"

"Usually you don't know what's going on. You can't always count on prospects to tell you the whole truth."

Carl laughed. "True enough, but maybe a little too tactful. Remember: Everything you say here is confidential. You can't get in trouble for telling me how you feel. So go ahead. What does the picture mean to you?"

Alan examined Carl's face with care. Was this a trap of some kind? "Honest? I can't get in trouble for telling you how I feel?"

"Honest," Carl replied. "That's one of the things Harvey sent you here to get better at. Saying what you feel, when you feel it."

Alan took a deep breath and then let it out. He sat up a little straighter in his chair. "In that case," Alan said, "how I feel is this: Prospects lie all the time."

"Good. Keep going."

"They lie the most at the very beginning of the relationship," Alan continued. "They lie somewhat less as the relationship moves forward. But there's never any way to know for sure whether they are lying to you, no matter how close they seem to get to you and no matter how strong the relationship seems." He wasn't quite sure how it had happened, but Alan was now standing up. His fists were clenched. He was breathing a little more heavily than before.

"You sound a little bitter."

Alan sat down again. He found himself thinking of that big account last month, the one he had lost without any warning whatsoever. "I'm fine," he said.

Carl must have known better. "Really?"

Alan stared at his fists. "No, not really. I'm not fine. I recently got burned by a current client who lied to me. Earlier this year, over lunch with her team, she told me that everything looked good. Then, last month, she switched to the competition. That was my biggest account. All the lunches I had taken her and her team out to over the years—and I still got burned. So yes, when I asked my contact how she felt things were going, I expected her to tell me the truth. I expected the whole picture. Maybe the moral of that story is: prospects lie. Current clients do, too."

Carl smiled. He uncapped a plastic marker and wrote these words, in large letters, across the drawing of the iceberg.

Everybody Lies

"It's not just prospects and customers, Alan. It's everybody. Sometimes it's a huge lie. Sometimes it's a little lie. Sometimes it's people not knowing what the heck they should say, and covering for that as best they can. For all I know, that's what happened with your vanishing customer. For all *you* know, that's what happened—since I'm guessing from Harvey's notes that you had only one real point of contact within that account. Am I right about that?"

Alan looked away, feeling sheepish. It was true. The woman he had sold to was in fact the only manager he had ever spoken to within that account. Harvey had never stopped harping about that, either—the need for multiple points of contact. Now that Alan stopped to think of it, he realized that one... two...no, all three of his remaining customers had only a single person he could call and talk to if a problem ever arose.

"I'll take that as a *yes*," Carl said. "Now listen, Alan. Most salespeople pretend that prospects are telling them the truth. It makes them feel better. The Contrarian Salesperson accepts the reality that everybody lies as a given, and then assumes personal responsibility for verifying and re-verifying everything he hears. It's kind of like what Ronald Reagan said in dealing with the Soviet Union. 'Trust, but verify.'

"If something goes wrong because of faulty or incomplete information, Contrarian Salespeople accept that as something they did wrong, not something the prospect or customer did wrong. In the same way a doctor doesn't take everything a patient says as literally true, a Contrarian

Salesperson accepts a professional responsibility to verify and evaluate information from multiple angles. Because everybody lies, at least a little."

> *"Everybody lies."*
>
> **—GREGORY HOUSE, MD**

"Wait a minute. You're telling me you lie, too?" Alan asked, wondering if perhaps the best defense was a good offense.

"Not if I can possibly avoid it. But if a six-year-old hands me a stick-figure drawing and says, 'Is my picture of you good?'—what do you think I'm going to say?"

Alan chuckled.

"Not only that. I regularly find myself out to eat at a restaurant, finishing a meal that I didn't particularly enjoy. Yet when the waiter comes up and asks how my meal was, I usually say 'It was good.' In fact, I find most people do that. If I'm having a bad day and someone asks me how I'm doing, I'll quite often say that I'm fine. We all do this. Who knows why?"

When Carl put it that way, it was a little easier to accept the idea that everybody lied from time to time.

"Lies are part of the human experience," Carl continued. "No matter how good your relationship with any one individual contact is, you still need to drill beneath the surface. Whatever that person tells you, gives you, or shows you, you have to assume you're not getting the whole story. Every issue you hear, every piece of information you uncover, is potentially untrue, misleading, or incomplete. It's your job—no one else's—to create enough background information, enough context, to get the complete picture.

"For instance, if you ask your best customer a question like, 'How are we doing?'—you have to be ready to confirm whatever it is you hear. The fact that you like the answer you hear first doesn't mean it's accurate."

"Kind of like the waiter asking you about the meal," Alan observed.

Carl smiled. "Yep. The point is, the issue you hear about at the first meeting may not be the real issue. The pain that the prospect wants to talk about with you may not be the real pain. The budget figure the prospect shares with you may not be the real budget. Prospects may even blow smoke about something like who the real decision makers are. At any point in the sales cycle, in any given conversation, the odds are good that you're only looking at part of the iceberg.

"They may even look you in the eye, lie, and tell you they are very interested in working with you just so they can get your proposal and your unpaid consulting."

Alan shook his head in dismay. "Getting accurate information seems pretty difficult."

"That's why we have 70/30 and the Rule of Three Plus."

"Why we have what?"

"The 70/30 principle," Carl explained, "says that you should be listening 70% of the time on the sales call and talking only 30% of the time. The only way to get the prospect talking is to ask good questions, right?"

"Right," said Alan. "So you can get below the surface of the iceberg."

"Exactly. Always remember: Your value as a salesperson is related to what you ask and not what you tell."

"So what's the Rule of Three Plus?" Alan asked.

"That principle," continued Carl, "says that it takes at least three questions on the same topic to get to the real issue—to get below the surface of the water, so you can see the rest of the iceberg. You know going in that people are going to mislead you. That doesn't make them evil, by the way. It just makes them human. Even current clients may mislead you about things like their budget or whether they are talking to the competition—as you saw for yourself! But remember: That wasn't the prospect's mistake. It was yours."

Alan pondered this. "How is that my fault again?"

"You didn't assume personal responsibility," Carl said.

"For what?"

"For asking the right people the right questions in the right way. Alan, one of your main jobs as a salesperson is to get information—not give information. Your value as a salesperson is related to what you ask, not what you tell."

Alan sat up a little straighter in his chair.

"Your goal," Carl continued, "is to provide a solution for this person if you know you can or walk away if you know you can't. That means your primary professional responsibility is to gather information, not give it away. Again: Think of what happens when you go to the doctor. Does she spend a lot of time telling you what medical school she graduated from? Or does she ask you the questions she needs to ask in order to make a good diagnosis?"

"Wow," said Alan. "I never thought of it that way."

"Practice the Rule of Three Plus this week. And while you're at it, write down the questions you should have asked that client of yours during that lunch. I'll see you next Saturday."

SUMMARY

Carl Contrario's Wisdom in a Nutshell

- Everybody lies.
- You should be listening 70% of the time on the sales call and talking only 30% of the time. The only way to get the prospect talking is to ask good questions.
- Your value as a salesperson is related to what you ask, not what you tell.
- It takes at least three questions on the same topic to get to the real issue—to get below the surface of the water so you can see the rest of the iceberg.
- Your goal as a sales professional is to get information, not give information.

The Traditional Salesperson:

1. Believes everything a prospect tells them.
2. Talks more than listens.
3. Accepts the first answer.

The Contrarian Salesperson:

1. Knows everybody lies.
2. Listens more than talks.
3. Drills down to get the real answer.

Carl's Question for You

- What improvements do you need in order to make your questioning more successful?

RULE 4

No Coasting

Kathy was standing behind the easy chair, rubbing Alan's shoulders as he sat watching TV. As usual, she could tell he was concerned about something.

"What's the matter, honey?" Kathy asked. "Something's bugging you. I can tell."

Alan sighed. "The garbage disposal is making weird noises. I'm afraid to find out how much it's going to cost to fix. Things are pretty tight this month."

Kathy nodded and kissed the top of his head from behind the chair. "I can do without a garbage disposal," she said. "It's no problem."

Alan chuckled, but rubbed his eyes. "It is a problem. I wasn't counting on another big bill."

Kathy came around the side of the easy chair and plopped herself into Alan's lap. She gave him a big grin. "Fortunately," she said, "I love you no matter what. The lean times are about to end. You've been doing everything that Carl has been telling you to do, right?"

Alan didn't answer right away.

"Well, have you?"

Alan sniffed. "What are you, my conscience all of a sudden?"

"Maybe."

Alan scoffed, then sat up a little straighter in his seat and looked around the room.

"Where's the remote?" he asked. "I want to turn this off and look over my notes before my session with Carl tomorrow."

Kathy dug the remote out of the seat cushion where Alan had left it and flicked off the TV. She kissed him on the head again. "I'm going to go clean out the minivan so you can drive it to your session with Carl tomorrow."

• • •

"So," Carl asked the following morning, "what did you implement?"

Alan consulted the scrawls on the little sheet he'd prepared the night before. "I have to warn you," he said. "It's not pretty. I told five prospects that I wasn't going to submit the information they wanted because they wouldn't share any information with me. All five said, 'OK, fine—we'll get a quote from someone else.' Oh, and that Adult-to-Adult thing you wanted me to do? I actually tried that with each of those prospects. One of them put me in my place. The 'asking questions' thing was really tough, too. I didn't get much meaningful information." Alan frowned. "That was my week. Whatever it is I'm doing, it's clearly not working."

Carl gave a big grin that seemed to Alan to be totally inappropriate. "You didn't really expect to master everything instantly, did you, Alan? It takes a while, you've got to give it some time. I can tell you're on the right track!"

"Thanks. I'm still way behind quota, though."

"Next up for people who are way behind quota," Carl announced briskly, "is Contrarian Salesperson Rule Number Four: No coasting. Simple enough, I think. I don't think we'll need to spend a lot of time on that one, do you?"

Carl reached into his desk, extracted a small aluminum sign that read, "No coasting," and handed it to Alan. He then stared at the struggling salesperson, as though the lesson were already self-evident.

Alan examined the sign with due reverence, then set it down

with care on the small table next to his overstuffed chair. "'No coasting,'" he said. "Am I supposed to know what that means?"

"It means," Carl explained with evident patience, "that I want you to be Paul Simon, instead of Herman's Hermits."

Alan waited for elaboration, but none was forthcoming. "Paul Simon as in Simon and Garfunkel?"

"Yes."

"OK. But don't you think you ought to explain who Herman's Hermits were? They're not really ringing a bell for me."

"Marvelous! Exactly! Perfect! You know who Paul Simon is! But you don't remember Herman's Hermits! You've got it! I knew you would be a quick study." Carl's face bore yet another strange, inappropriate smile. "We can move right on to Rule Number Five, then. In Rule Number Five, the main thing to remember is..."

"Wait a minute!" Alan shouted. "I'm not ready for Rule Five! I've still got some work to do here!"

Carl nodded, and made a little note on a scrap of paper on his desk. Though it was upside down, Alan was still able to read it because it was in big letters:

Knows he still has work to do.
He's not coasting.

"Marvelous," Carl said, his face beaming. He underlined the words "not coasting." "Marvelous."

"Well, OK," Alan said. "I do have some work to do here. Forgive me for pressing the point, but what in the world do you mean by 'no coasting'?"

"I, Alan," Carl said slowly, "am Henry VIII. Make sense now?"

The air in the room felt denser than usual with mystery.

"I'm afraid not," Alan answered.

"In August of 1965," Carl said, standing, and beginning to pace about the room, "Herman's Hermits had the number one song in America. It was called 'I'm Henry VIII, I Am.' Perhaps you've heard of it?"

Alan sat back and thought. His dad had listened to a lot of 1960s songs on the oldies station when Alan was growing up, and that catchy tune, a kind of dopey English music-hall romp, did seem familiar now. "Yes. I've heard of it."

"A novelty hit, more or less. And Herman's Hermits' last one. They tried and failed to generate hits from the same grab-bag of effortless, irreverent whimsy. In other words, they failed at the task of reinventing themselves. They stopped growing. With me so far?"

Alan nodded.

"Five months later," Carl continued, "in January of 1966, the debut single from Simon and Garfunkel hit number one in the States. That song was called 'The Sound of Silence.' Paul Simon wrote it. Have you heard of that?"

"Of course."

"And?"

"And what? I still don't see where you're going with this."

Carl stopped pacing and fixed Alan dead in the eyes. "Two songs, two number one hits. One was written by a coaster. Not a member of the Coasters, mind you. I mean, a band that ends up trying to live the same one year of experience 5 or 10 or 20 or 30 years in a row. That's coasting. That's failure to reinvent yourself. It kills you, you know.

"The other song was written by an explorer, someone who refused to stand still, someone who was launching a great career based on constant reinvention. That career is still paying dividends, nearly five decades later because it was based on him challenging himself to do what he had never done before."

"Hmm," said Alan.

"Paul Simon challenged himself to explore new territory, not the same patch of ground over and over and over. He's marvelous. I do mean that literally. You look at the man and you can't help but marvel at what he's accomplished. Whether it's rock, or folk, or reggae, or world music, or even more recent trends nobody can label, he's still reinventing himself, and he's still ahead of the curve. Marvelous!

"So which one do you want to be, Alan? A coaster? Someone who finds a plateau where he can go to sleep and stays there? Or an explorer, like Paul Simon? Someone who keeps challenging himself to reach new personal heights? Someone who's marvelous?"

Another silence filled the room.

"Don't you see, Alan? You have to be the one to decide which kind of career you want. I certainly can't decide for you. You might as well decide now."

"Paul Simon," Alan said.

"You sure?"

"Absolutely. Hey, wasn't it Paul Simon who wrote, 'He who is not busy being born is busy dying'? Because that would seem to tie in here, right?'"

> **"He who is not busy being born is busy dying."**
>
> **—BOB DYLAN**

"It does fit," said Carl Contrario. "But that was Bob Dylan. Equally marvelous, though. Speaking of marvelous undertakings, have you ever climbed Mount Everest, Alan?"

Not quite certain where the conversation was going, Alan did what he had by now learned to do whenever Carl changed the subject. He followed Carl's lead. "No, Carl, I haven't."

"Do you want to?"

"Do I want to climb Mount Everest? Um...maybe someday."

"For the sake of argument, let's pretend you do. Don't worry. This is just a game. I won't hold you to it. Shall we play?"

"Sure."

"Remind me. What's your goal?"

"To get to the top of Mount Everest."

"How high up is that, do you think?"

"I have no idea."

"29,029 feet. How high would you say you want to go if your aim is to climb to the top of Mount Everest?"

"29,029 feet—obviously."

"Marvelous. You've definitely got the hang of this game. Now let me ask you this: How do you think the view is going to be when you start the climb at Base Camp—which is 17,700 feet above sea level?"

"I expect it would be OK."

"How about halfway into the climb, at a place called Camp 3, which is 23,625 feet above sea level? That view would be tremendous; one of the best views in the entire world. You could get used to that view, couldn't you? You could see for miles from Camp 3. You might decide to hang out at Camp 3 for a while. In fact, you might even stay in your tent, stay warm with your portable stove, and forget you ever even wanted to get to 29,029 feet.

"The difficulty is, Alan, a lot of people are pretty happy with the view from Camp 3. Some people spend their whole careers camping out halfway up the mountain—and even more people spend their careers at the foot of the mountain, staring up, wishing that they could start climbing to 29,029 feet. Translated to the world of sales, this means that there are some people who could be doing a whole lot better than they are—but they get stuck in their comfort zone."

"Comfort zone," Alan said. "I remember back in high school, when I was lifting weights. My coach used to talk about comfort zones all the time."

"Yes. It's a behavioral space where your activities are consistent with your existing beliefs."

Alan was puzzled. "Is a comfort zone really all that bad? Isn't it good to have a place where you're comfortable sometimes?"

Carl shook his head. "They call it a comfort zone for a reason, Alan. It's comfortable there. But if it's so comfortable it stops us from moving forward toward a goal that's important to us, that's something we need to notice.

"Operating in your comfort zone minimizes stress and risk but it also limits growth. Ultimately, human beings aren't wired to be happy, or fulfilled, without big goals. When you stop halfway up the mountain, you don't have a big goal anymore. The point is to be willing to stretch beyond your comfort zone. If you're not stretching, you're not growing. If you're not growing, you're dying."

"Back to Bob Dylan again," Alan said.

As though he had not even heard the previous remark, Carl said, abruptly: "Tell me. Do you like swimming?"

Alan didn't miss a beat this time. "Yes," he said. "I do like swimming."

"Me too. It's my favorite form of exercise. In fact, there's a river not far from here where I go for my workouts once a week. I always swim upstream."

"Sounds invigorating," said Alan.

"It is. It's challenging, swimming upstream. In life, we all know there's going to be a current running against us from time to time. When you're swimming in a river, it's OK to tread water once in a while. If you decide to tread water for too long, though, there's a problem. You might get used to that. You know what happens when you get used to treading water? Eventually, you find yourself floating downstream."

Alan nodded and took some notes on his pad of paper. When he looked back up, Carl was studying him intently.

Alan said, "So far I've got the Billboard listings for late 1965, Mount Everest, and swimming against the stream of a river."

"Let me ask you directly," Carl said. "Are you committed to finding new ways to reinvent yourself as the need arises, so that you don't ever become complacent? Are you ready to be Paul Simon?"

"Yes," Alan said. "I am. I don't want to coast through my career."

"Marvelous! What's your big goal? What's the top of Mount Everest for you, Alan?"

The answer came to Alan with surprising ease. "My wife Kathy was an art history major in college," he said. "She's always talking about going on a vacation to Florence. I'd like to be able to take her to Italy on a nice, long, leisurely holiday. Oh, and I want to buy her a BMW. With cash. Not loans."

"Anything else?"

"Yeah," said Alan. "I want to fix the darn garbage disposal in the kitchen."

"Good. Then since we know where you're going, you're ready to move on. See you next week. Remember, there's no such thing as try. You're going to implement the things we've been talking about, including the Rule of Three Plus. Right?"

"Right!"

SUMMARY

Carl Contrario's Wisdom in a Nutshell

- No coasting.
- Don't tread water for long.
- Don't get stuck in your comfort zone.
- Make an ongoing commitment to reinvent yourself and keep striving for important goals.
- If you're not busy being born, you're busy dying.

The Traditional Salesperson:

1. Stays in the comfort zone.
2. Is easily satisfied.
3. Does the same thing over and over.

The Contrarian Salesperson:

1. Pushes beyond the comfort zone.
2. Achieves big goals and then sets new, bigger goals.
3. Is always learning and growing.

Carl's Questions for You

- Are you in a comfort zone? If so, what do you need to do to get out of it?

RULE 5

Manage Behavior, Not Results

"Asking a bunch of questions actually doesn't come that easy to me," Alan told his boss Harvey at their weekly Friday check-in. "All those iceberg questions Carl wants me to ask—I mean, I'm trying. It's just not that comfortable for me."

Harvey sat back in his chair and looked at Alan for a long moment. "Not comfortable?" Harvey asked. "That's what you said?"

"Yes," Alan said. "I'm sure he means well, though."

"Not comfortable?" Harvey repeated. "Do you want to be

comfortable at this point in your career, Alan? Because if I were you, honestly, I'd want to get as uncomfortable as I could possibly get right now. He did talk to you about comfort zones, right?"

Alan winced. "Yeah," he said, giving a little nod. "I guess he did go over that."

"Is it possible you haven't accepted the idea of doing something new?" Harvey asked. When Alan hesitated, Harvey said, "Let me ask you this. Are you absolutely sure you want to make more money?"

Alan looked at him as though he were speaking a foreign language. "Of course I want to make more money."

"Really?" Harvey said. "If you wanted to make more money, wouldn't you have done so already?"

Things got very quiet in Harvey's office.

"Have a good session tomorrow," Harvey said, smiling. "And check your messages. Juan at the front desk told me someone from Consolidated Consumer Services called and just left you a message."

•   •   •

Carl Contrario extracted a newspaper from his desk drawer, unfolded it, handed it to Alan, and asked: "Where did he crash?"

"Where did who crash?"

Carl glanced downward at the headline. Alan scanned it dutifully.

Driver Injured in Horrific Race Crash

Beneath the headline was a color photograph of a crumpled race car. "The driver, Alan. Where did he crash?"

"Against that big wall. Obviously."

"Nope."

Alan hated trick questions. "OK, I give up. Where did he crash?"

"Picture your career as a car on a racetrack. You're the driver. You crash. The question is, where did you crash? Did you crash when you hit the wall? Or did you crash somewhere else?"

The discussion seemed to have taken a metaphysical turn, one Alan found a little irritating. He knew, however, that Carl must have some point in mind, and that the point in question was likely to have something to do with whatever he was supposed to do if he wanted to replace the garbage disposal, get to Florence, and buy his wife a BMW. So Alan said, "I don't know, Carl. Where else would I have crashed if I didn't crash at the wall?"

"You crashed way before here." Carl drew an X on the curve's outside wall, where the car hit, and then drew an O to mark a spot well before it. "You didn't crash at the X point. You crashed at the O point."

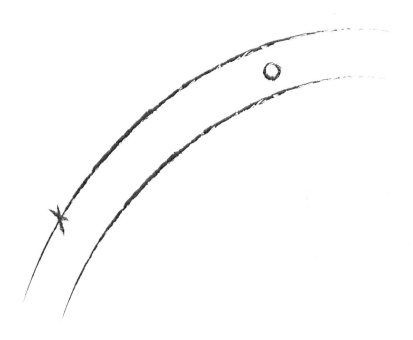

Alan peered at the illustration, puzzled. "All the way back there?"

"Now can you tell me why?"

Alan moved through the track in his head. "Because I had to get ready for the curve."

Carl slapped the desk. "Marvelous! Because you had to get

ready for the curve." He placed a big check mark next to the O he had made on the pad. "Think about that. If you're doing 235 miles an hour in the straightaway, and you're still going 235 miles an hour when you reach that curve, that means you stopped paying attention back here, where I marked the O. That's the point where you should have gotten ready to adjust your speed. And you didn't. You didn't even check what was right in front of you, right in your windshield, while you still had time to take action. At that point, you could have hit the brakes, downshifted, turned your wheel—but none of that will help now. It's too late. You've already crashed back here at the beginning of the curve, Alan. Hitting the wall is just a confirmation of that."

"I get it."

"Great. Explain it to me."

"The results aren't happening where we think they are happening. They're happening much earlier."

"Marvelous! Most salespeople sit behind their desks on, say, December 31. What do they do? They check the fourth-quarter sales results and think, *Oh, gosh, it's December 31. I didn't make my quota.* All they see is the crumpled car. But guess what? That's the X point I marked on the track. If you have a bad quarter on December 31, where does that happen? Depending on your sales cycle, it could have happened back in September or June or March. Salespeople need to be tracking their metrics all the way back at the O point.

"An example would be something like, say, the ratio of calls made to conversations with prospective new opportunities. By the way, do you know what that number is for you for the past month?"

"For me, personally?"

Carl looked at him.

Alan shifted uneasily in his chair. "All I'm counting right now is the deals I close."

"If all you do is count how many sales you close, you're begging for a disaster. You're looking at where you've been, not where you're going. You're heading for the wall without giving yourself time to adjust."

"It's OK to know how many deals I close, though, right?"

"Of course. But that's a lagging indicator. What you want to count is a leading indicator, like conversations with new people. It's all about looking at the right stuff early enough to give yourself a picture of where you're going. You've got to give yourself time to adjust. Otherwise, you're going to hit the wall. That's not a prediction, Alan. That's a guarantee."

"Got it," said Alan.

"Marvelous! So Rule Five is: 'Manage behavior, not results.'"

SAMPLE LEADING INDICATOR RATIOS

- *Attempted calls that turn into conversations with new prospects*
- *Conversations that lead to appointments*
- *Appointments that lead to proposals*
- *Proposals that lead to closed sales*

Alan was still puzzled. "Why should I have to track a whole lot of data, though? I mean, I've been doing this for a while. I know what it takes to make a sale happen."

"I'm sure you do," Carl said, "but even so, I promise you, there are early indicators you should be tracking also. Aren't you the tiniest bit curious? For example, wouldn't you like to know how many conversations it takes you to get an appointment? Let's say it takes you ten conversations to set one appointment. That's good to know! Now you have a benchmark from which to improve. How are you going to know whether you're getting any better if you don't know what you're doing now?"

"I guess that does make sense," Alan said.

"So let me ask you, Alan—when's the point in your calendar when you decide whether or not you're going to make your annual quota on December 31?"

Alan thought for a moment.

"No later than the first of June," Alan said. "Which would mean that I've already crashed."

"Indeed you have," Carl said, the vaguest outline of a smile forming on his lips. "But by the time we get done next Saturday, you're going to be out of trouble—and back on track. That's what happens to Contrarian Salespeople who manage their behavior."

SUMMARY

Carl Contrario's Wisdom in a Nutshell

- Manage behavior, not results.
- The results aren't really happening where you think they're happening. They're happening much earlier.
- Track leading indicators, not just lagging indicators.
- Give yourself time to change behaviors and affect the most important outcomes.

The Traditional Salesperson:

1. Manages results.
2. Has no time to adjust.
3. Focuses on sales, not behavior.

The Contrarian Salesperson:

1. Manages behavior.
2. Has time to adjust.
3. Tracks behavior and knows ratios.

Carl's Question for You

- What leading indicators should you be tracking?

RULE 6

Use a Sales Process

Diego Difficult, VP of Purchasing for Consolidated Consumer Services, stood and shook Alan's hand. As Diego did so, he had an expression of puzzlement on his face. "Well, thank you for telling me in person, Alan," Diego said. "It's really not what I expected."

"I know," Alan said. "But I do think this is what makes the most sense for both of us."

• • •

At the start of the next session, Alan told Carl excitedly, "We're getting somewhere. I'm getting more second meetings, and what I'm learning with you is helping change the dynamic. This week I declined the opportunity to quote on a job where there were nine other bidders: Consolidated Consumer Services. I realized our company has been pursuing this lead for years. We've never seen a nickel out of it. I went in and told my contact there that we were going to pass. I felt great about that."

"Bravo! What did your contact say when you told him that?"

"He looked at me a little funny. He said he'd talk to the boss and let me know what she says. Maybe that will happen, maybe it won't. But I'm not jumping through that particular hoop. By the way, that discussion got me thinking about the whole Adult-to-Adult thing we've been talking about. I came up with an idea about how we might run this week's session."

"What's that?" asked Carl Contrario, pouring himself tea from a Thermos bottle he had produced from the lowest desk drawer. "Care for a cup of tea?"

"No, thank you," Alan said. "Suppose, this time around, you tell me what the rule is before you start telling me some kind of weird story or metaphor or riddle about it?"

"Why would I want to do that?" Carl asked, peering over

the sturdy metal cup he had placed before his lips. He took a long sip.

"Because," Alan explained patiently, "that way I might get a clearer sense of what is supposed to happen during the discussion. Then we might both know what's actually going on. Ahead of time. For a change."

"Knowing what's going on ahead of time, for a change," Carl repeated, dreamily. "Yes. I do believe that's important. You know what? I'll do it. This is the perfect rule for you and I to have an equally clear idea about what, exactly, is going on. There should be absolutely no mystery when it comes to Rule Six." Carl took another thoughtful sip of the tea from the cup. He stared at the ceiling calmly. He seemed in no particular hurry to do anything.

Finally Alan asked: "So what is it?"

"So what is what?"

"The rule we will be looking at next. What is that?"

"Oh." said Carl. "That." He drained the rest of his cup, screwed it back deftly onto the top of the Thermos, and replaced it in the drawer. "Rule Six is: 'Use a sales process.' Or, if you prefer, 'Knowing what is actually going on, ahead of time, for a change.'"

Alan grimaced. "I had a feeling something like this was coming. Process orientation. Not my strong suit."

Carl smiled. "Tell me, what do you think it is that makes so many salespeople unhappy about identifying and following a process? That's not a trick question. You can answer it honestly."

Alan sat back in his chair. "I suppose," he answered at last, "it's because 'identifying and following some process,' as you put it, feels a little bit like being given a set of handcuffs. Or even worse, like a prison sentence. Like I'm being punished for something."

"I can certainly understand that," Carl said. "In fact, at the beginning of my career, I used to feel exactly the same way. 'Don't handcuff me! Let me do my job!' I'm sure I said that at some point, or something similar to it. What do you say when your boss tries to get you to show him evidence that you follow a process?"

"I told him I was smart enough to do my job without a lot of handholding."

"Hmm," Carl said. "You used those words?"

Alan nodded. "He's big on checklists, but they drive me nuts. This one I was supposed to be following made me fill in blanks about the 'purpose of the discussion.' The 'problems' I should be identifying. Pain, he called it. What 'objections' I should expect. What my responses would be. Things like that. Anyone who's been selling for more than a month and has common sense at all knows all of that stuff ahead of time, without having to fill out a checklist."

Feeling as though he had struck a long-overdue blow for the autonomy of salespeople everywhere, Alan smiled a little and straightened up in his seat, eagerly anticipating Carl's next move. "The thing Harvey needed help understanding," Alan continued, "is that I've got my own checklist. It's all common sense. And it's all up here." He tapped on his temple.

"Interesting. Did you say anything else about 'common sense' to your boss along those lines?"

"I did! I told him, 'If you didn't think I was smart enough to do the job without that checklist, then why did you hire me?' That's when he started looking at me funny." Alan frowned. "Come to think of it, that might have been the moment he decided to put me on notice."

"Yes," said Carl. "I should say, though, in the interests of full disclosure, that I said something very similar to my first sales boss—before he fired me."

"You? Fired?"

"Another story for another day, perhaps. But I'm curious: What, specifically, makes you think that smart people don't need checklists?"

A silence fell over the room. Alan was not quite sure how to break it.

"For instance," Carl pressed, "would you say that I'm a smart person?"

Finally. An easy question. "Yes," Alan said. "I would classify you as a smart person."

"Why, thank you! I think you're smart, too. Now, would it interest you to know that I am a qualified skydiver with over a hundred successful jumps?"

Alan regarded Carl's slim, wiry frame and pictured it in a skydiving suit, hurtling through an open sky, with a parachute deploying gracefully above. It was surprisingly easy to do. "Yes," Alan said. "That's very interesting!"

"Good. How many of those hundred jumps do you think I made without using a checklist?"

Alan saw where this was going. He tried to buy some time by saying, "Not many."

"Try zero."

"OK, zero."

"Right. Ask me why."

Alan decided evasion was useless. "Why?" he asked.

"Because I'm smart, Alan. A smart person doesn't rely on common sense in a stressful situation."

Alan shifted uneasily in his seat, and then said, "Maybe I'm no skydiver."

"Maybe. After all, It's not your life we're talking about. It's

your livelihood that's at stake here. Or maybe there is a con-
nection. You never know. Next question: Are airline pilots
smart?"

"I sure hope so."

"If you flew on a plane, would you want the pilot to use a
checklist before starting the engine and taking off?"

There was another awkward pause. "Yes. Look. I do get
your—"

"Are doctors smart? If you had to go in for brain surgery,
would you want the doctor to follow a checklist?"

"All right, all right."

"If a doctor is smart enough to do the job—and surely the
doctor who makes it through medical school has some claim
to being smart—why would you want to handcuff him with
a checklist?" Carl sipped his tea as Alan braced himself. Sure
enough, Carl said: "Let me tell you a story."

Alan groaned.

Carl didn't seem to notice. "Some highly skilled people
at Johns Hopkins University Hospital in Baltimore wanted
to decrease the number of patient fatalities from infections.
They took a close look at their intensive care unit.

"They came up with a checklist. All the items that were
on that checklist were things that any doctor (or any medical
student, for that matter) should know to do. For instance:

Wash your hands with soap and clean the patient's skin with antiseptic. There were five simple tasks the surgeons were supposed to follow.

"As I say, the doctors already knew they were supposed to complete all five tasks before beginning surgery. Even so, the management of the hospital turned that list of five tasks into a checklist. Pretty simple, right?"

Alan agreed. "Common sense."

"The tricky part about common sense, Alan, is the difficulty of following it at the moment it's needed. If you asked the surgeons at that hospital whether they were already doing all five of those things, what answer would you think you would have gotten?"

"I'd expect them to say 'yes.'"

"They probably thought things like: *We don't need a checklist. We're already doing that. By the way, we're smart. Don't handcuff us.* But the hospital management pressed the point. They clamped down. They got everyone to agree to follow the checklist, and they posted that checklist in the ICU."

"So what happened?"

> "The problem with common sense is that it's not all that common."
>
> **—WILL ROGERS**

"Nurses observed the doctors for a month. In more than a third of patient cases, the doctors skipped at least one of the five items on the list, even though the doctors were smart—and had lots of common sense.

"The story's not over. The hospital's executives gave nurses permission to stop doctors if they noticed them skipping one of the steps. Guess what happened? The ten-day line infection rate went from 11 percent of surgeries to zero percent of surgeries. The hospital figured that over a 15-month period, they had prevented 43 infections, and they kept eight people from dying, as a result of having buy-in on that checklist. So what's our point here, Alan?"

Alan pondered that one for a moment, and then said, "If you ever have to go to an ICU, make sure it's the one at Johns Hopkins?"

Carl chuckled. "Try again."

"Checklists aren't really a set of handcuffs."

"Not unless you make them into handcuffs," Carl said. "Even smart people need checklists to deliver great results. Doctors have a lot of things to remember. So do pilots. So do people who jump out of airplanes. And so do you. It's probably going to come as no surprise to you that your boss shared a copy of the checklist he wants you to work with before you go on a sales call. I'd like you to take another look at it."

Carl handed Alan a form. It looked like this.

PRE-CALL CHECKLIST	
	1. What is your objective for the meeting?
	2. What is the reason the prospect invited you in? (problems, frustrations, delays, waste, losses, etc.)?
	3. What agenda did you set on the phone? Did you send it in writing/email?
	4. What research have you done?
	5. What questions will they have of us? How are we going to respond?
	6. What objections will they have of us? How are we going to respond?
	7. What pain questions are you planning on asking? What tools will you use to get more pain? What pains did you discover in previous meetings (if you have had them)?
	8. What type of budget do you think they will have or have you uncovered already?
	9. What is a typical decision-making process in other companies like theirs? What is the cast of characters?
	10. What do you want the outcome to be?
	11. Are we going to role-play before the call?

"Of course, you're smart, Alan. Of course, you've got common sense. Of course, you know what you're doing. That's why you were hired in the first place. But what I want you to do when you get back to work is to start thinking of this sheet a little like the checklist in that ICU. That sheet could keep you from making a mistake that could kill your patient—the deal.

"There's a lot to remember in the operating room. There's a lot to remember in an airplane. And there's a lot to remember during a sales call. The more people who know what's going on, the more people who know what process is being followed, the better. Because when everything's coming at you from all directions, you want some kind of process in place, just in case you miss a step. Fair enough?"

"Fair enough." Alan said.

> *"Selling is what takes place when you lead the prospect through a step-by-step process... each step of which may lead to the prospect's disqualification and removal from the process."*
>
> **—DAVID H. SANDLER**

SUMMARY

Carl Contrario's Wisdom in a Nutshell

- "Common sense" is a disaster waiting to happen.
- Use a checklist.
- No one's common sense is good enough to make a checklist obsolete.
- Be process oriented.
- Get regular input from other people about your process orientation.

The Traditional Salesperson:

1. Wings it.
2. Doesn't prepare.
3. Doesn't believe in process.

The Contrarian Salesperson:

1. Has a process.
2. Uses a pre-call checklist.
3. Knows "Process makes me stronger."

Carl's Questions for You

- Are you following a documented sales process? What should be on your pre-call checklist?

RULE 7

Embrace Deliberate Practice

"How's it going at work?" Kathy asked Alan.

"It's going OK," Alan said. "Carl wants me to make all these extra calls now. I'll be all right. But it's tough. This is one of the most difficult things I've ever done."

Kathy didn't say anything for a few moments.

"What?" Alan asked. "What is it?"

"Is what he's asking you to do actually working? Are your numbers better now?"

Alan didn't even have to think about the answer to that. "Yes," he said. "The numbers are definitely better."

"Nice!" Kathy said. "When you say it's tough, though—tough compared to what? You could be overseas in the military. Or you could be homeless. Or you could be out of food. Is what you're doing tough compared to any of that?"

Alan turned and looked at her. "What are you trying to say, honey?" he asked.

"Nothing," Kathy said. "Except I know you're actually a pretty tough guy."

• • •

At the beginning of the next session, after replaying what he'd implemented in the week just past, Alan watched in awe as Carl Contrario got up from his desk, found a corner of the room that appeared to agree with him, and stood on his head, his palms flat against the floor.

"Let's look at things a little differently on this next rule, Alan," he said, his upside-down face looking surprisingly untroubled. "That's a hint, by the way. A big one. I want you to change the way you look at your job."

Alan braced himself.

"If you were to ask a hundred successful CEOs whether truly great salespeople are born or made," Carl continued, "how many do you think would say that they're born?"

"Most of the CEOs, I guess," Alan said. "That seems to be the prevailing attitude."

"Indeed it does." Carl exited his headstand and sat deftly in the lotus position on a spot in the exact middle of the floor. "My experience is that the majority of those hundred CEOs would give that answer. Sometimes it's because they think of themselves as born salespeople. Just out of curiosity, Alan, are you one of your company's top sales performers right now?"

"Of course, I'm not. If I were, why would I be here?" Alan said. "But in a good year, I'm not far from it. Right now, though, I'm not even in the middle. I'm in the bottom fifth of producers for this year. I guess I'm in trouble. I've heard some mutterings from the people in Human Resources. Paula Procedure, for instance. She thought I couldn't hear her talking on her cell phone once, but I could while I was in the break room and she was in the hall. She was telling one of her colleagues that I'm just not cut out for sales because I rank low on the chart right now. She also said she suspected me of being a closet introvert, meaning an introvert who hides being an introvert. She doesn't think introverts make good salespeople. Supposedly, they're not cut out for sales."

"'Not cut out for sales,'" Carl repeated. "Is that what you think missing quota means? Not being cut out for the job?"

"It's what a lot of people seem to think it means," Alan answered.

"Is that why Harvey sent you here? To turn you into a 'born salesperson'?"

Alan had no answer.

Carl got up to resume his customary position behind his desk. "It's plain foolish to believe that motivated salespeople in the bottom fifth of any team can't move up to the top fifth. I did. You're just about to do the same thing. It's just as foolish to believe introverts can't become great salespeople. I've helped hundreds of introverted salespeople to do just that. It's not so much whether you are an introvert or an extrovert that matters, but whether you can communicate effectively with introverts and extroverts."

"A study published in Psychological Science...debunks the widely-held belief that extroverts make better salespeople than introverts. The study found that extreme extroverts and extreme introverts get just about the same (not great) results—and that the people who get the best sales results are those who can flex between introverted and extroverted behavior."

—ERIKA ANDERSON,
"The Unexpected Secret to Becoming a Great Salesperson," Forbes.com, April 12, 2013

Carl pulled out, from the top drawer of his desk, a photograph of Tiger Woods in his prime, celebrating one of his PGA tournament wins. He showed it to Alan. "You recognize this guy?"

"I do. I'm a big golf fan."

"Some people say he's one of the greatest golfers who ever lived."

"Yep," Alan said. "I'm one of those people."

"So am I," said Carl. "So we're in agreement on that much. Tell me: Was Tiger Woods born great, or was he made great?"

Alan hesitated. Given what he had just heard, he suspected that this was a trick question. He waited for Carl to say something, which, fortunately, he did.

"It's true that there's no one else like Tiger Woods," Carl said. "It's true that he had success very early in life. He won his first tournament at age eight. But that doesn't mean he came out of the womb preprogrammed for victory on the golf course. If he had, he wouldn't have had to do any practicing at all, would he? But what do we know about Tiger Woods?"

"He's a fiend for practice."

"Now we're getting somewhere. Yes. Tiger Woods is a fiend for practice. In fact, he's a fiend for a certain kind of practice. It's known as 'deliberate practice.' Deep expertise has more to do with how you practice than it does with just performing a familiar skill a bunch of times.

"Someone who becomes expert in a certain area—say, golf—does bring certain genetic advantages to the table. Height, for instance. There's never been a PGA champion who was three feet tall. But that's not all that has to happen for someone like Tiger Woods to rise to the top of the game. He had to break down all the specific skills that are required for excellence and to focus relentlessly on improving those skills through practice and role-play."

"Role-play?"

"Tiger hits a special kind of sand trap shot in practice, for instance. Usually, when a ball lands in the sand trap, it sits on the top of the sand. Very rarely, though, the ball comes in on a line drive and ends up half-buried in the sand. Despite the rarity of this, Tiger practices by dropping balls in the sand trap, stepping on them, and then hitting them out with each ball half-buried in the sand. He has hit hundreds of those kinds of shots."

"Wow."

"He might only have to make a sand trap-shot like that— with only the top of the ball showing, looking kind of like the yolk of a sunny-side up egg—once or twice during an entire PGA season. But when it does happen, he's got a huge body of practice that he's invested in handling the situation. And he's saved a stroke."

"So—isolate the situations that matter, and drill your responses to those like crazy," said Alan.

"There's more. People who do this kind of practice are much more likely to get immediate feedback from a coach. Tiger does that, of course, and he always has. Not only that— people like Tiger practice continually, and they practice at more and more challenging levels, with the intention of developing mastery."

"How much do I have to practice?"

"Most of the people who've studied all of this closely agree that the kind of mastery we're talking about—Tiger's level— only happens after about 10,000 hours of focused practice."

"Wow. That's a lot of hours."

"It is. People like Tiger Woods have two big advantages when it comes to logging those 10,000 hours: a supportive family environment and a desire to succeed, no matter what their age is. In Tiger's case, we know he was introduced to golf by his dad Earl before he was two years old, and we also know Earl was his first great coach. A coach makes all the difference. Tiger's dad was athletic, a college baseball star, and a single-figure handicap amateur golfer. But first and foremost, he was his son's coach."

"If he hadn't taken on that role, would Tiger have discovered his passion for golf?"

"Hard to say. What we know for sure is that Earl Woods spent a whole lot of hours on the golf course with his son, enough to win him a special appearance on national television as a 'child prodigy' before he even turned three. But sometimes that 'child prodigy' label is a little misleading, like the 'born salesperson' label."

"Which means?" Alan asked.

"Look, Alan," Carl said briskly, looking Alan straight in the eye. "Whether you're two years old, 22 years old, or 62 years old, either you have a coach or you don't. Either you do put in those countless hours of practice, or you don't. Either you commit to mastery in your chosen field or you don't.

"Here's where I'm going with this: Do you want an ongoing coaching relationship with me, a relationship where we meet once a week for an hour to work on your personal development plan? Or don't you?"

Alan felt his neck tensing up. One of the things he'd always liked most about being a salesperson was the feeling that his time was his own, that he wasn't accountable to anyone for his plans. Yet clearly, that approach hadn't worked out too well for him.

Carl was waiting. "Well?"

Something inside Alan whispered, *Go ahead and say, "Yes."*

"Yes," Alan said. The tension in his neck vanished.

"Good," said Carl. "But I don't want you to be under any misunderstanding. The fact that you've got a coach doesn't mean the coach is responsible for your deliberate practice. You're the one who's responsible for that. You've gotten a good start today, but you need to make a commitment to me and to yourself that you're willing to keep that momentum going. Do we have a deal?"

"Yes," Alan agreed again.

"Good. Now, please understand: What we're talking about here is a daily pattern of self-development and training. That's a lot more than listening to a CD once and then thinking, *I've got it.* Or going to a one-time seminar and saying 'Great, I'm fixed!'"

Alan nodded, extended his hand, and said, "We've got a deal, Carl."

"Marvelous!" Carl shook Alan's hand and held on to it. "To summarize: I'm assuming you are committed to investing time, every day, on the skill sets that matter the most. We're going to start with your qualifying skills because the simplest way to double your business is to improve your ability to qualify whether a prospect has the pain, the budget, and the necessary decision process to work with you. That's basic blocking and tackling, Alan, and you need to get better at it. Agreed?"

"Agreed," said Alan.

"You're going to need to put in effort every working day, starting this week," Carl continued. "I'd recommend you aim for two hours a week of deliberate practice, including role-plays, in addition to our weekly one-hour coaching sessions on Saturday. Are you up for that?"

Alan considered this proposal. He wasn't crazy about role-plays. Carl seemed to sense his hesitation.

"Alan, can you think of a professional sport where they only practice once in a while?"

Alan couldn't.

"It doesn't exist. Not if they're any good. What you've just agreed to is a professional commitment, and it needs a professional schedule. Two hours during the working week and an hour on Saturday is the minimal professional commitment for salespeople I coach. You can make that commitment—or you can make no commitment at all. Either one is fine with me. If you decide it's no commitment, and we're done here, I'm OK with that. I just need to know."

Alan thought it over, then nodded vigorously. "I'm in," he said. "Two hours during the week and an hour on Saturday."

Carl shook Alan's hand once more. "Marvelous," said Carl.

"Marvelous. And remember Rule Seven: 'Embrace deliberate practice.'"

SUMMARY

Carl Contrario's Wisdom in a Nutshell

- You can practice during the game or before the game—the choice is yours.
- Even if you once underperformed, you can and will move up—once you embrace the principle of deliberate practice and are motivated enough to stick to it.
- Introverted salespeople are just as capable of delivering great sales results as extroverted salespeople.
- Role-play is a vitally important part of deliberate practice for salespeople.

The Traditional Salesperson:

1. Practices during the sales call.
2. Looks for quick fixes to improve sales skills.
3. Works independently.

The Contrarian Salesperson:

1. Practices before the sales call.
2. Embraces deliberate practice and ongoing personal growth.
3. Works with a coach.

Carl's Questions for You

- What improvements do you need to make to your practicing? How much time are you spending on personal growth when it comes to your sales skills? Who is your coach?

RULE 8

If You Feel It, Say It

A lan was in Harvey's office, and a big grin was on his face. "You're never going to believe what happened," Alan said.

"What?" Harvey asked, looking up from his computer screen.

"You remember Consolidated Consumer Services? The lead we've been chasing for years? Without winning so much as a dime in revenue?"

"Yeah?"

"The one I told my contact we weren't going to bid on?"

"Yeah?"

"Last week, the president of the company called me up and asked me what I needed to see in order for us to put together a bid," Alan said. "I told him that we would need to meet in person to discuss what his organization's needs were. He wanted me to respond via email, but I pushed back and sent him a message saying that if we didn't have a face-to-face meeting, it wouldn't make any sense to go any further. To make a long story short, I met with him, and I closed the deal. We got the account! And it's huge!"

Harvey stood and applauded. Alan smiled and bowed.

"So," Alan said, as Harvey shook his hand. "I guess this means I'm across the finish line!"

Harvey looked at him quizzically. "Across the finish line?" Harvey asked. "What do you mean?"

"Well," Alan said, "doesn't this sale put me as far above quota now as I've ever been?"

"Yes. And?"

"Well, I thought that, given the circumstances, I might be able to stop these little debrief sessions we've been having after each of my weekend meetings with Carl."

Harvey shook his head slowly. "You were in the room when he was talking to you about deliberate practice, weren't you?" Harvey asked.

Alan thought for a bit, and then nodded. "Yes. Yes, I was."

Harvey clapped his hands together and then pointed right at Alan. "Good," Harvey said. "Have a great session tomorrow. Can't wait to hear how it goes."

•   •   •

When Alan showed off the brochure for the BMW he and Kathy were planning to buy next quarter—giving her unrestricted access to the minivan at last—Carl was all smiles.

"It won't be long until you're driving one of those."

"According to my projections, three months, maybe sooner," said Alan.

"Have you done a test drive yet?" Carl asked. "You won't know what it's really like until you drive it."

"Yep," said Alan. "And now I know exactly why I need to keep my total conversations and my qualified presentations up. My wife picked the model out. She's got a thing for BMWs."

"She's got good taste," Carl said.

"I like to think so." Alan said. "Anyway, it beats taking a cab. I'm finally making enough to make some positive changes in my lifestyle. I thought: What better way to remind myself of what I'm capable of than to test drive a BMW?"

Carl nodded. "Fair enough," he said. "It's important to

have goals. If a BMW goal works for you—great! Now, I've got one more suggestion to share with you."

"The eighth rule? I've been wondering about that. What is it?"

Carl pointed to a poster on the wall, one that he must have put up at some point during the previous week. Alan had never seen it before.

> *"If you feel it, say it."*
>
> **—DAVID H. SANDLER**

The poster read: "Rule Eight: 'If you feel it, say it.'"

"Do what most salespeople won't do," said Carl. "Be the contrarian. Say what you're feeling. If there's an issue that's bothering you, something that might affect what happens in the sale, bring it up yourself. Say what you feel about it. Think of this as being authentic. I'll give you an example. Can you call to mind a prospect you talked to recently?"

"Sure. Jim Mahoney. We had our first meeting yesterday."

"Was there anything that bothered you about that discussion?"

"Well—yeah. He asked if we had delivery from the plant within three weeks. Week after week, at every sales meeting, I get told not to build anything shorter than four weeks into a proposal. There's just no way I can give it to him."

"What did you say to Jim about that?"

"Um...nothing, really. I said I'd look into it."

"Why did you say that?"

"I guess I didn't want to look bad."

"So, you're saying that getting Jim to like you was more important than figuring out whether the two of you could do business together."

There was a silence as Alan thought about this. "It doesn't make a lot of sense when you put it that way."

"This is another one of those habits I want you to walk away from, Alan: needing to be liked. Whenever you sell, you're playing a kind of game. You get to set the rules of this game. So, you might as well set the rules up in a way that allows you to say what you feel without getting hurt. After all, this isn't even a friend or a close family member. This is someone you're trying to qualify and with whom you're building a business relationship. Either there is a reason for you two to do business together or there isn't. If the discussion doesn't end the way you hoped it would, that's too bad—but it's no judgment on you as a person. It can't be because Jim doesn't know you that well, right?"

Alan pondered this for a moment. "Right," he said. "It can't be."

"Think of some other games you play in life. You're the same person before you play a round of golf as you are afterwards. Your value as an individual, as a human being, doesn't go up or down based on the outcome of that golf game, does it?"

"No," said Alan, his voice strengthening. "No, it doesn't."

"If it's just a game, and if you get to set the rules of the game, why not say how you're feeling?"

Alan said, "Huh."

"Something to think about," Carl said, smiling.

> *"No one can make you feel inferior without your consent."*
>
> **—ELEANOR ROOSEVELT**

"But what should I have said?" Alan asked.

"Assuming you think there might be a problem with getting delivery as quickly as he wants," Carl said, "at the very least, bringing the problem up yourself makes it easier for you to handle the potential objection, rather than having to handle it while you're on the defensive. So, why not tell him you're struggling with that part of the discussion because you're concerned it might lead to problems later on?

"You can apply this strategy to any part of the sale where you might reasonably expect to encounter a problem or disagreement. That might be delivery, it might be financing, it might be creditworthiness, it might be inventory status or pricing. You name it. If your experience tells you that there's a real possibility of you and the prospect experiencing a bump in the road, you need to find a way to talk about it ahead of time and tell the prospect how you feel. When in doubt, say you're struggling and ask for help."

"I would just come right out and tell him I'm worried about this delivery thing?"

"It's easier than you think. I would say 'struggling,' instead of 'worrying,' though."

"OK. Here goes." Alan took a deep breath and plunged in. "'Jim, I've been struggling with something we talked about last time. You mentioned you were wanting delivery within three weeks of the time you place the order. It turns out we can't provide that. It's going to take at least four. Is that going to be a problem?'"

The words felt confident and assured as they came out of Alan's mouth. He had no problem at all picturing himself saying something like this to a prospect now.

"Perfect," said Carl.

"That was easy. And it sounded great. Why didn't I try this years ago?"

"Because you were afraid of the same thing all the other

salespeople are afraid of: looking bad. But you can't let the fear of looking bad stop you from addressing the most important issues. You will only look more professional in the prospect's eyes by saying how you feel.

> *When in doubt, say you're struggling and ask for help.*

"Here's another example. Let's say you've been working on a proposal for someone. You call the prospect to talk about it, and you don't get a call back. Then you call the prospect the next week, wait a few days, and you still don't get a call back."

"I'm thinking they probably lost interest."

"Right. So what's wrong with calling and leaving a message that says that?"

"I don't know. I guess I don't want to sound negative."

"It doesn't have to sound negative. Listen to this: 'Bill, I've tried a few times to get in touch with you, and I haven't heard back. I'm thinking you've decided to go in a different direction and I should close your file. What I don't want to do is turn into a pest by continuing to call you if working together isn't right for you. If that's the case, I have no problem with you calling me up and telling me that. Unless I hear from you, I'm going to go ahead and close your file."

Alan pondered this. It made perfect sense. "If that's what's going on," Alan said, "why not come out and say it?"

"Saying how you feel doesn't make every problem vanish. But it shows you what you're up against, and it allows you to address any issues you may see that could be upsetting or bothersome to either party, now and in the future. Too often, salespeople think they're being honest, but what they're actually being is inauthentic. They hold back. They don't say what's on their mind because they're too busy trying to be nice. They're trying to avoid tension in the way they bring something up. Being inauthentic kills sales! The best sales calls always have moments of tension—like the one just now with the prospect who fell out of touch. Contrarian Salespeople welcome those moments. They're the moments where we learn what's really going on."

SUMMARY

Carl Contrario's Wisdom in a Nutshell

- If you feel it, say it.
- Don't let the fear of looking bad or losing momentum with the prospect stop you from addressing the most important issues.
- The best sales calls have moments of tension.

The Traditional Salesperson:

1. Holds back.
2. Avoids moments of tension.
3. Is inauthentic.

The Contrarian Salesperson:

1. Shares what's on his mind.
2. Welcomes moments of tension.
3. Says what he feels.

Carl's Questions for You

- Where in your sales process can you use the "If you feel it, say it" rule? Is there one account you work with now where you could use this rule? If so, which one?

The Best Present

Friday night. The kids were off at their grandparents' house for the weekend. Alan and Kathy had just gotten back from a day on the town—Alan had taken the whole day off. They'd gone to a museum. They'd gone to a nice restaurant. They'd gone to a play. They came into the kitchen now, and Kathy was holding Alan's hand.

Alan said, "Happy anniversary, honey."

Kathy took a look around. Her eyes came to rest on the kitchen table. Suddenly, her face was radiant. On the table were two first-class tickets to Florence, Italy.

Kathy let out a wordless shout of joy, and threw her arms around him. "Happy anniversary to you, too, baby! When do we leave?"

"Next Friday," Alan said. "If that's convenient. Your folks have agreed to watch the kids."

"Convenient!" Kathy shouted. "It's perfect!" Somehow the memory of struggling to pay for the new garbage disposal seemed quite distant. "That's not the best present you ever gave me, though."

"No? What is the best present?"

"Since you started working with Carl, I notice you're listening to me more," she said. "You're less stressed. It's easier to have a conversation with you at the end of the day. You're more engaged, more connected. And you're getting along with the kids better. More excited about the things they're doing. Something has changed."

She gave him a big kiss. All of a sudden, Alan was quite glad the kids weren't home.

After Florence

Once he got back from Florence, Alan kept working with Carl.

1. He zigged when others zagged. He looked at things differently. He questioned his own cherished assumptions about buying and selling.

   (Most salespeople do whatever the competition does and look to confirm what they already believe about selling.)

2. Alan stopped jumping through hoops. He no longer assumed his job demanded that he do everything a

prospect instructed. He kept his communication with prospects on an Adult-to-Adult level.

(Most salespeople do anything prospects tell them to do, which is hardly a peer-to-peer relationship.)

3. He stopped assuming that prospects were telling him the truth—and he stopped blaming prospects when they misled him.

    (Most salespeople talk more than they listen and don't question effectively.)

4. He made an ongoing commitment to reinvent himself, to keep striving toward important goals, and to move beyond his comfort zone.

    (Most salespeople stay in their comfort zone.)

5. He tracked his leading indicators along with his lagging indicators and gave himself time to adjust when necessary.

    (Most salespeople track only the deals they close or those that are in the pipeline.)

6. He started using and discussing the checklists his boss Harvey set up for him.

    (Most salespeople are not process oriented.)

7. He committed to a weekly coaching routine with Carl, embraced the principle of deliberate practice, and

spent significantly more time on role-plays with both Carl and Harvey.

(Most salespeople do not invest time in personal development and push back when they're asked to take part in role-play sessions. They practice on the actual sales call.)

8. He kept on saying what he felt, in conversations with prospects and his boss (and his wife!) and encouraged others to share how they felt.

(Most salespeople are too scared to say what they feel.)

It took some work to follow the eight principles of the Contrarian Salesperson, but with Carl's help, Alan stuck with it until it became second nature. He was mighty glad he did.

The Deal

"You've helped me a lot," Alan said to Carl one Saturday. "More than I imagined you could. I want to thank you."

Carl's famous grin was gone in an instant. His face went grey and cold. Alan could not remember him ever looking as severe. "Not yet, you don't."

Uh-oh, thought Alan.

"Are we finished yet?" Carl asked.

"Um...no?"

"Of course we're not! Have you started helping Harvey with onboarding new salespeople yet? Have you started sharing the Contrarian Selling Rules with other salespeople? Have you gotten your colleagues to the same place you're at now? Some of them still imagine that a few short meetings with a manager will be enough to turn everything around, you know."

Alan thought of how insistent Harvey had been that the lessons weren't over yet. "So I guess it isn't time to say 'thank you' yet?"

"No! Because you didn't give back yet! Graduates always give back, Alan. Go help someone implement the Contrarian Selling Rules. Then come back and say how grateful you are. That's the only 'thank you' I accept. Deal?"

"Deal!" said Alan.

"Marvelous!" said Carl. The big grin was back. "Marvelous!"

EPILOGUE

Alan did not become the Angel of Death's 100th victim. To the contrary, Paula Procedure offered to take Alan and Kathy out to dinner at the restaurant of their choice in celebration of his securing the top spot in the company's year-end rankings of salespeople. They accepted her offer.

"I really don't know how you did it, Alan," Paula said over filet mignon, "but you pulled off the only successful escape from a termination session I've ever seen. Congratulations. Here's to you." And she raised her glass in a toast. Alan clinked her glass and smiled. It was a particularly fine vintage of champagne. The food was delicious. The ambiance was perfect. Best of all, Paula was paying.

Alan kept up his coaching sessions with Carl, just as he'd promised. He kept meeting with Harvey once a week, too. He not only held on to his job, but he also emerged as a consistent top producer at Acme, year after year.

Which brings us to this morning. Over coffee, as the day began, Harvey asked Alan to mentor an acquaintance of his, Wendy Weakcloser, on the neglected sales science of zigging when other salespeople zagged. What did Alan think of that possibility?

"That's a *marvelous* idea, Harvey," Alan said. "I'd be happy to meet with her. Please ask Wendy to give me a call. Just don't expect me to schedule the meetings for Sunday morning. That's my new tee time."

THE EIGHT RULES OF
THE CONTRARIAN SALESPERSON

1. *Zig When Others Zag*

2. *Sell Adult-to-Adult*

3. *Everything Is an Iceberg*

4. *No Coasting*

5. *Manage Behavior, Not Results*

6. *Use a Sales Process*

7. *Embrace Deliberate Practice*

8. *If You Feel It, Say It*

AUTHOR'S NOTE

The principles shared in *The Contrarian Salesperson* are key concepts of the Sandler Selling System methodology.

With the purchase of this book, you have access to a complimentary seminar!

Take this opportunity to personally experience the non-traditional, Contrarian sales training and reinforcement coaching that has been recognized internationally for decades.

Sandler Training works with companies in the Fortune 1000 as well as thousands of small- to medium-sized businesses and nonprofits. Leaders in these organizations choose

Sandler for sales, leadership, management, and a wealth of other skill-building programs.

Now it's your turn, and it's free!

You'll learn the latest practical, tactical, feet-in-the-street sales methods directly from your neighborhood Sandler trainers. They're knowledgeable, friendly, and informed about your local selling environment.

Here's how you redeem your free seminar invitation.

1. Go to www.Sandler.com and click on Find Training Location (top blue bar).

2. Select your location.

3. Review the list of the Sandler trainers in your area.

4. Call your local Sandler trainer, mention *The Contrarian Salesperson* and reserve your place at the next seminar!

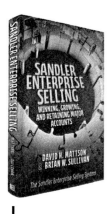

Our latest book addresses the specific issues of selling in the enterprise arena...

Sandler Enterprise Selling
Winning, Growing, and Retaining Major Accounts

Competitively pursuing large, complex accounts is perhaps the greatest challenge for selling teams. To keep treasured clients and gain new ones, you need a system to win business with profitable enterprise clients, serve them effectively and grow the relationships over time.

You start with Sandler Enterprise Selling. The only enterprise selling system based on the proprietary Sandler Selling System methodology created by David H. Sandler. This practical, step-by-step book is designed specifically for selling teams committed to high achievement in the enterprise environment. The program's powerful six stages will guide you to:

1. **Set a baseline for success** for each territory and account.
2. **Identify opportunities** with the highest probability of success.
3. **Engage with buyers** to qualify enterprise opportunities.
4. **Craft solutions** that directly address your client's needs.
5. **Propose** your solution and achieve advancement.
6. **Serve and satisfy your client,** earning the right to grow the business.

Win enterprise business and learn how to respond to changing sales dynamics

Sandler Training®

BIBLIOGRAPHY

Anderson, Erica, "The Unexpected Secret to Becoming a Great Salesperson," Forbes.com, April 12, 2013

Gawande, Atul, *The Checklist Manifesto: How to Get Things Right,* Picador (London), 2011

Sandler, David, *You Can't Teach a Kid to Ride a Bike at a Seminar,* McGraw-Hill (New York), 2015

ACKNOWLEDGMENTS

To the Sandler Home Office, for their support (and patience) through the process of this book. In particular, Dave Mattson, for the opportunity to share the contrarian story with the world.

For making this book happen, literally, Yusuf Toropov.

For ongoing love and support, Herb, Renee, and Keith Brauer.

For help with ideas and feedback on this book: Greg Powell, Kevin Grogan, Ken Harris, Jeff Christensen, Chris Hammond, Russell Grissett, Dean Dietrich, Dean Engelage, Ron Haub, Dan Miller, Frank Stewart, Mark Greenhill, Dave

Jenner, Randy Walkowiak, Bill Bartlett, Dennis Mellott, Maurice Forde, Dave Mattson, Dan Sullivan, Lee Brower, Myron Byronski, Georgie Weeble, Markku Kauppinen, Marshall Goldsmith, and, last but certainly not least, Bill, Mike, Michael, and Peter.

For support and feedback from Mastermind Groups past and present: John Rosso, Karl Scheible, Mark McGraw, Matthew Neuberger, David Clegg, Gerry Weinberg, Steve Taback, Gary Harvey, Paul Lushin.

For a truly great team I have the privilege of working with every day: John Martin, Jim Mattei, Karen James, Ernie Giarelli.

For those who are feeling bad because I left you out, sorry about that. Thanks also.

CONTINUE THE DISCUSSION

For more information about
Sandler Training, visit us at:

www.sandler.com

ALSO FROM SANDLER TRAINING

Accountability the Sandler Way (Knox)
Bootstrap Selling the Sandler Way (Morrison)
Customer Service the Sandler Way (MacKeigan)
Five Minutes with Vito (Mattson/Parinello)
Lead When You Dance (Mattson)
LinkedIn the Sandler Way (LinkedIn/Sandler Training)
Prospect the Sandler Way (Rosso)
The Sales Coach's Playbook (Bartlett)
Sandler Enterprise Selling (Mattson/Sullivan)
The Sandler Rules (Mattson)
Sandler Success Principles (Mattson)
Selling Technology the Sandler Way (Chiarello)
Selling to Homeowners the Sandler Way (Booker/Doyle)
Selling Professional Services the Sandler Way (Polin/Polin)
Succeed the Sandler Way (Scheible/Boyd)
Transforming Leaders the Sandler Way (Arch)
You Can't Teach a Kid to Ride a Bike at a Seminar (Sandler)

Available at:
www.sandler.com/resources/sandler-books